Jesus is Missing

Blessing Obada

WestBow Press books may be ordered through booksellers or by contacting:

WestBow Press
A Division of Thomas Nelson & Zondervan
1663 Liberty Drive
Bloomington, IN 47403
www.westbowpress.com
844-714-3454

ISBN: 978-1-6642-4776-5 (sc)
ISBN: 978-1-6642-4777-2 (e)

Library of Congress Control Number: 2021921502

Print information available on the last page.

WestBow Press rev. date: 11/02/2021

WestBow
PRESS®
A DIVISION OF THOMAS NELSON
& ZONDERVAN

Jesus is Missing

DEDICATION

Dedicated to D1 and D2.

Jesus is Missing where is he ? Is a question we all ask at some time in our lives. This book echoes this question in this delightful children's book that brings the question back to the Easter Story with the heart of a child that is searching for Jesus and being comforted by the fact that he is not missing but very much alive today and always.

I wholly recommend this enchanting book by Blessing Obada.

Georgia Vaitl BA CPCC PCC
Professional life and relationships Coach.

Daddy daddy
Come with me!

Jesus is missing
Where is he?
Oh no!

Neighbour neighbour
Have you heard?

Jesus is missing
Join the search.
Eek! Eek!

Tailor tailor
Close your shop!

Jesus is missing
What a shock.
Zoom! Zoom!

Cobbler cobbler

Take a break!

Jesus is missing
So they say.
Quick! Quick!

Mason mason
Drop your hose!

Jesus is missing

Off we go.

Zap! Zap!

Vendor vendor
Turn your cart!

Jesus is missing

This is sad.

Boo hoo!

People people
Please don't cry!

He's not missing

He's alive!

Ah! Ah!

Let's be happy
Let's be glad

Jesus lives
In our hearts
Yay! Yay!

Happy Easter
Everyone
This is Easter
Oh what Joy!!!
Hooray!!!

APPRECIATION

Praise be to God for his gifts and endowments.
Thanks to my dear friends Gloria Vaitl,
Susan Wenz and Laurie Martin who took the
time to read, comment and show support.
Not forgetting Ngozi Okwuosa and ArtDan
for their excellent creativity and tips.

Finally, I deeply appreciate my family, for all the
inspiration, love and support. God bless you!

Printed in the United States
by Baker & Taylor Publisher Services